BRITISH POETS SERIES

I0109145

William Shakespeare: *Selected Sonnets and Verse*
edited, with an introduction by Mark Tuley

Edmund Spenser: *Poems*
selected and introduced by Teresa Page

Robert Herrick: *Selected Poems*
edited and introduced by M.K. Pace

John Donne: *Poems*
selected and introduced by A.H. Ninham

D.H. Lawrence: *Selected Poems*
edited with an introduction by Margaret Elvy

Percy Bysshe Shelley: *Poems*
selected and introduced by Charlotte Greene

Thomas Hardy: *Selected Poems*
edited, with an introduction by A.H. Ninham

Emily Bronte: *Poems*
selected and introduced by Teresa Page

John Keats: *Selected Poems*
edited with an introduction by Miriam Chalk

Henry Vaughan: *Poems*
selected and introduced by A.H. Ninham

The Crescent Moon Book of Love Poetry
edited by Louise Cooper

The Crescent Moon Book of Mystical Poetry in English
edited by Carol Appleby

The Crescent Moon Book of Nature Poetry From Langland to Lawrence
edited by Margaret Elvy

The Crescent Moon Book of Metaphysical Poetry
edited and introduced by Charlotte Greene

The Crescent Moon Book of Elizabethan Love Poetry
edited and introduced by Carol Appleby

The Crescent Moon Book of Romantic Poetry
edited and introduced by L.M. Poole

Blinded By Her Light The Love-Poetry of Robert Graves
by Jeremy Robinson

The Best of Peter Redgrove's Poetry: The Book of Wonders
by Peter Redgrove, edited and introduced by Jeremy Robinson

Peter Redgrove: Here Comes the Flood
by Jeremy Robinson

Sex-Magic-Poetry-Cornwall: A Flood of Poems
by Peter Redgrove, edited with an essay by Jeremy Robinson

Brigitte's Blue Heart
by Jeremy Reed

Claudia Schiffer's Red Shoes
by Jeremy Reed

By-Blows: Uncollected Poems
by D.J. Enright

*Shakespeare: Love, Poetry and Magic
in Shakespeare's Sonnets and Plays*
by B.D. Barnacle

Love For Love:
Selected Poems

Love For Love:
Selected Poems

Sir Thomas Wyatt

Edited by Louise Cooper

CRESCENT MOON

CRESCENT MOON PUBLISHING
P.O. Box 393
Maidstone
Kent, ME14 5XU
United Kingdom

First published 1994. Second edition 2008
Introduction © Louise Cooper, 1994, 2008.

Printed and bound in Great Britain.
Set in Garamond Book 12 on 15pt.
Designed by Radiance Graphics.

The right of Louise Cooper to be identified as the editor of *Selected Poems: Love For Love* has been asserted generally in accordance with sections 77 and 78 of the Copyright, Designs and Patents Act 1988.

All rights reserved. No part of this book may be reprinted or reproduced, stored in a retrieval system, or transmitted, in any form or by any means, electronic, mechanical, photocopying, recording or otherwise, without permission from the publisher.

British Library Cataloguing in Publication data

Wyatt, Sir Thomas
Love For Love: Selected Poems. – (British Poets Series)
I. Title II. Cooper, Louise
III. Series
821.2

ISBN 1-86171-124-7
ISBN-13 9781861711243

CONTENTS

POEMS ATTRIBUTED TO THOMAS WYATT

Allington Castle, Maidstone, Kent, where Thomas Wyatt was born and lived.

Go, burning sighs, unto the frozen heart.
Go break the ice which pity's painful dart
Might never pierce; and if mortal prayer
In heaven may be heard, at last I desire
That death or mercy be end of my smart.
Take with thee pain whereof I have my part
And eke the flame from which I cannot start,
And leave me then in rest, I you require.
    Go, burning sighs.
I must go work, I see, by craft and art
For truth and faith in her is laid apart.
Alas, I cannot therefore assail her
With pitiful plaint and scalding fire
That out of my breast doth strainly start.
    Go, burning sighs.

If amorous faith in heart unfeigned,
A sweet languor, a great lovely desire,
If honest will kindled in gentle fire,
If long error in a blind maze chained,
If in my visage each thought depainted,
Or else in my sparkling voice lower or higher
Which now fear, now shame, woefully doth tire,
If a pale colour which love hath stained,
If to have another than myself more dear,
If wailing or sighing continually,
With sorrowful anger feeding busily,
If burning afar off and freezing near
Are cause that by love myself I destroy,
Yours is the fault and mine the great annoy.

My heart I gave thee, not to do it pain;
But to preserve, it was to thee taken.
I served thee, not to be forsaken,
But that I should be rewarded again.
I was content thy servant to remain
But not to be paid under this fashion.
Now since in thee is none other reason,
Displease thee not if that I do refrain,
Unsatiate of my woe and thy desire,
Assured by craft to excuse thy fault.
But since it please thee to feign a default,
Farewell, I say, parting from the fire:
For he that believeth bearing in hand,
Plougeth in water and swoeth in the sand.

I find no peace and all my war is done.
I fear and hope, I burn and freeze like ice.
I fly above the wind yet can I not arise.
And naught I have and all the world I seize on.
That looseth nor locketh, holdeth me in prison
And holdeth me not, yet can I scape no wise;
Nor letteth me live nor die at my device
And yet of death it giveth me occasion.
Without eyen I see and without tongue I plain.
I desire to perish and yet I ask health.
I love another and thus I hate myself.
I feed me in sorrow and laugh in all my pain.
Likewise displeaseth me both death and life,
And my delight is causer of this strife.

The lively sparks that issue from these eyes
Against the which ne vaileth no defence
Have pressed mine heart and done it none offence
With quaking pleasure more than once or twice.
Was never man could anything devise
The sunbeams to turn with so great vehemence
To daze man's sight, as by their bright presence
Dazed am I, much like unto the guise
Of one ystricken with dint of lightning,
Blinded with the stroke, erring here and there.
So call I for help, I not when ne where,
The pain of my fall patiently bearing.
For after the blaze, as is no wonder,
Of deadly 'Nay' hear I the fearful thunder.

Unstable dream, according to the place
Be steadfast once or else at least be true.
By tasted sweetness make me not to rue
The sudden loss of thy false feigned grace.
By good respect in such a dangerous case
Thou brought'st no her into this tossing mew
But madest my sprite live my care to renew,
My body in tempest her succour to embrace.
The body is dead, the sprite had his desire;
Painless was th'one, th'other in delight.
Why then, alas, did it not keep it right,
Returning to leap into the fire,
And where it was at wish it could not remain?
Such mocks of dreams they turn to deadly pain.

You that in love find luck and abundance
And live in lust and joyful jollity,
Arise for shame, do away your sluggardy,
Arise, I say, do May some observance!
Let me in bed lie dreaming in mischance,
Let me remember the haps most unhappy
That me betide in May most commonly,
As one whom love list little to avance.
Sephame said true that my nativity
Mischanced was with the ruler of the May.
He guessed, I prove of that the verity:
In May my wealth and eke my life, I say,
Have stood so oft in such perplexity.
Rejoice! let me dream of your felicity.

Sighs are my food, drink are my tears;
Clinking of fetters such music would crave.
Stink and close air away my life wears.
Innocency is all the hope I have.
Rain, wind, or weather I judge by mine ears.
Malice assaulted that righteousness should save.
Sure I am, Brian, this wound shall heal again
But yet, alas, the scar shall still remain.

Lover: It burneth yet, alas, my heart's desire.
Lady: What is the thing that hath inflamed thy heart?
Lover: A certain point, as fervent as the fire.
Lady: The heat shall cease if that thou wilt convert.
Lover: I cannot stop the fervent raging ire.
Lady: What may I do if thyself cause thy smart?
Lover: Hear my request and rue my weeping cheer.
Lady: With right good will. Say on. Lo, I thee hear.

Lover: That thing would I maketh two content.
Lady: Thou seekest, perchance, of me that I may not.
Lover: Would God thou wouldst, as thou mayst
                                well, assent.
Lady: That I may not. Thy grief is mine, God wot.
Lover: But I it feel, whatso thy words have meant.
Lady: Suspect me not. My words be not forgot.
Lover: Then say, alas, shall I have help or no?
Lady: I see no time to answer. Yea. But no.

Lover: Say yea, dear heart, and stand no more in doubt.
Lady: I may not grant a thing that is so dear.
Lover: Lo, with delays thou drives me still about.
Lady: Thou wouldest my death. It plainly doth appear.
Lover: First may my heart his blood and life bleed out.
Lady: Then for my sake, alas, thy will forbear.
Lover: From day to day thus wastes my life away.
Lady: Yet, for the best, suffer some small delay.

Lover: Now, good, say yea. Do once so good a deed.
Lady: If I said yea, what should thereof ensue?
Lover: An heart in pain, of succour so should speed.
          'Twixt yea and nay my doubt shall still renew.
          My sweet, say yea and do away this dread.
Lady: Thou wilt needs so. Be it so. But then be true.
Lover: Naught would I else, nor other treasure none.

Thus hearts be won by love, request, and moan.

The knot which first my heart did strain
When that your servant I became
Doth bind me still for to remain
Always your own, as now I am;
And if ye find that I do feign,
With just judgment myself I damn
   To have disdain.

If other thought in me do grow
But still to love you steadfastly,
If that the proof do not well show
That I am yours assuredly,
Let every wealth turn me to woe
And you to be continually
   My chiefest foe.

If other love or new request
Do seize my heart but only this,
Or if within my wearied breast
Be hid one thought that mean amiss,
I do desire that mine unrest
May still increase and I to miss
   That I love best.

If in my love there be one spot
Or false deceit or doubleness
Or if I mind to slip this knot
By want of faith or steadfastness,

Let all my service be forgot
And, when I would have chief redress,
   Esteem me not.

But if that I consume in pain
With burning sighs and fervent love
And daily seek none other gain
But with my deed these words to prove,
Methink of right I should obtain
That ye would mind for to remove
   Your great disdain.

And for the end of this my song,
Unto your hands I do submit
My deadly grief and pains so strong
Which in my heart be firmly shut.
And when ye list, redress my wrong
Since well ye know this painful fit
   Hath last too long.

The joy so short, alas, the pain so near,
The way so long, the departure so smart!
The first sight, alas, I bought too dear
That so suddenly now from hence must part.
The body gone, yet remain shall the heart
With her, which for me salt tears did rain,
And shall not change till that we met again.

Though time doth pass, yet shall not my love.
Though I be far, always my heart is near.
Though other change, yet will not I remove
Though other care not, yet love I will and fear.
Though other hate, yet will I love my dear.
Though other will of lightness say adieu,
Yet will I be found steadfast and true.

When other laugh, alas, then do I weep.
When other sing, then do I wail and cry.
When other run, perforced I am to creep.
When other dance, in sorrow I do lie.
When other joy, for pain well near I die.
Thus bought from wealth, alas, to endless pain,
That undeserved, causeless to remain.

Like as the swan towards her death
Doth strain her voice with doleful note,
Right so sing I with waste of breath,
'I die! I die! and you regard it not.'

I shall enforce my fainting breath
That all that hears this deadly note
Shall know that you doth cause my death.
'I die! I die! and you regard it not.'

Your unkindness hath sworn my death
And changed hath my pleasant note
To painful sighs that stop my breath.
'I die! I die! and you regard it not.'

Consumeth my life, faileth my breath.
Your fault is forger of this note,
Melting in tears a cruel death.
'I die! I die! and you regard it not.'

My faith with me after my death
Buried shall be, and to this note
I do bequeath my weary breath
To cry 'I died and you regarded not.'

What means this when I lie alone?
I toss, I turn, I sigh, I groan.
My bed me seems as hard as stone.
    What means this?

I sigh, I plain continually.
The clothes that on my bed do lie
Always methink they lie awry.
    What means this?

In slumbers oft for fear I quake.
For heat and cold I burn and shake.
For lack of sleep my head doth ache.
    What means this?

A mornings then when I do rise
I turn unto my wonted guise,
All day after muse and devise.
    What means this?

And if perchance by me there pass
She unto whom I sue for grace,
The cold blood forsaketh my face.
    What means this?

But if I sit near her by
With loud voice my heart doth cry
And yet my mouth is dumb and dry.
    What means this?

To ask for help no heart I have.
My tongue doth fail what I should crave.
Yet inwardly I rage and rave.
    What means this?

Thus have I passed many year
And many a day, though naught appear
But most of that that most I fear.
    What means this?

At most mischief
I suffer grief,
For of relief
Since I have none
My lute and I
Continually
Shall us apply
To sigh and moan.

Naught may prevail
To weep or wail.
Pity doth fail.
In you, alas.
Mourning or moan,
Complaint or none,
It is all one
As in this case.

For cruelty
Most that can be
Hath sovereignty
Within your heart,
Which maketh bare
All my welfare.
Naught do ye care
How sore I smart.

No tiger's heart
Is so pervert
Without desert
To wreak his ire.
And you me kill
For my good will!
Lo, how I spill
For my desire!

There is no love
That can ye move
And I can prove
None other way.
Therefore I must
Restrain my lust,
Banish my trust
And wealth away.

Thus in mischief
I suffer grief,
For of relief
Since I have none
My lute and I
Continually
Shall us apply
To sigh and moan.

Since ye delight to know
That my torment and woe
    Should still increase
    Without release,
I shall enforce me so
That life and all shall go
For to content your cruelness.

And so this grievous train
That I too long sustain
    Shall sometime cease
    And have redress
And you also remain
Full pleased with my pain
For to content your cruelness.

Unless that be too light
And that would ye might
    See the distress
    And heaviness
Of one yslain outright,
Therewith to please your sight
And to content your cruelness.

Then in your cruel mood
Would God forthwith ye would
    With force express
    My heart oppress

To do your heart such good
To see me bathe in blood
For to content your cruelness!

Then could ye ask no more.
Then should ye ease my sore
And the excess
Of mine excess.
And you should evermore
Defamed be therefore
For to repent your cruelness.

from "Lo, what it is to love!"

Love is a fervent fire
Kindled by hot desire;
    For short pleasure
    Long displeasure.
Repentance is the hire,
    A poor treasure
    Without measure.
Love is a fervent fire.

O goodly hand
Wherein doth stand
My heart distressed in pain!
Fair hand, alas,
In little space,
My life that doth restrain!

O fingers slight,
Departed right,
So long, small, so round,
Goodly begone
And yet alone
Most cruel in my wound.

With my lilies white
And my roses bright
Doth strive thy colour fair.
Nature did lend
Each finger's end
A pearl for to repair.

Consent at last,
Since that thou hast
My heart in thy demesne,
For service true
On me to rue
And reach me love again.

And if not so
Then with more woe
Enforce thyself to strain
This simple heart,
That suffereth smart,
And rid it out of pain.

What death is worse than this?
     When my delight,
My weal, my joy, my bliss
     Is from my sight
     Both day and night,
My life, alas, I miss.

For though I seem alive
     My heart is hence.
Thus, bootless for to strive
     Out of presence
     Of my defence,
Toward my death I drive.

Heartless, alas, what man
     May long endure?
Alas, how live I then?
     Since no recure
     May me assure,
My life I may well ban.

Thus doth my torment go
     In deadly dread.
Alas, who might live so,
     Alive as dead,
     Alive to lead
A deadly life in woe?

Ye know my heart, my lady dear,
That since the time I was your thrall
I have been yours both whole and clear
Though my reward hath been but small.
So am I yet and more than all.
And ye know well how I have served
As, if ye prove, it shall appear:
　　How well, how long,
　　How faithfully,
　　And suffereth wrong
　　How patiently.
Then since that I have never swerved
Let not my pains be undeserved.
Ye know also, though ye say nay,
That you alone are my desire
And you alone it is that may
Assuage my fervent flaming fire.
Succour me then, I you require.
Ye know it were a just request,
Since ye do cause my heart, I say,
　　If that I burn
　　That ye will warm
　　And not to turn
　　All to my harm,
Sending such flame from frozen breast
Against all right for my unrest.

And I know well how forwardly
Ye have mista'en my true intent
And hitherto how wrongfully
I have found cause for to repent.
But if your heart doth not relent,
Since I know that this ye know,
Ye shall slay me all wilfully;
 For me and mine
 And all I have
 Ye may assign
 To spill or save.
Why are you then so cruel a foe
Unto your own that loves you so?

Poems attributed to Thomas Wyatt

My love is like unto th' eternal fire
And I as those which therein do remain
Whose grievous pains is but their great desire
To see the sight which they may not attain.
So in hell's heat myself I feel to be
That am restrained by great extremity
The sight of her which is so dear to me.
O puissant love and power of great avail
By whom hell may be felt or death assail!

O miserable sorrow withouten cure!
If it please thee, lo, to have me thus suffer,
At least yet let her know what I endure
And this my last voice carry thou thither
Where lived my hope now dead forever;
For as ill grievous is my banishment
As was my pleasure when she was present.

At last withdraw your cruelty
    Or let me die at once.
It is too much extremity,
    Devised for the nonce,
    To hold me still alive
    In pains still for to strive.
    What may I more sustain,
    Alas, that die would fain
    And cannot die for pain?

For to the flame wherewith I burn
    My thought and my desire,
When into ashes it should turn
    My heart by fervent fire
    You send a stormy rain
    That doth it quench again
    And makes my eyes express
    The tears that do redress
    My life in wretchedness.

Then when these should have drowned
    And overwhelmed my heart
The heat doth them confound,
    Renewing all my smart.
    Then doth the flame increase.
    My torment cannot cease.
    My pains doth then revive
    And I remain alive

With death still for to strive.

But if that you will have my death
    And that you would no other,
Then shortly for to stop my breath
    Withdraw the one or other,
    For this your cruelness
    Doth let itself, doubtless,
    And that is reason why
    No man alive nor I
    Of double death can die.

My sweet, alas, forget me not
That am your own full sure possessed;
And for my part, as well ye wot,
I cannot swerve from my behest.
Since that my life lieth in your lot,
At this my poor and just request
    Forget me not.

Yet wot how sure that I am tried,
My meaning clean, devoid of blot.
Yours is the reproof: ye have me tried
And in me, sweet, ye found no spot.
If all my wealth and health is the good,
That of my life doth knit the knot,
    Forget me not.

For yours I am and will be still
Although daily ye see me not.
Seek for to save that ye may spill
Since of my life ye hold the shot.
Then grant me this for my goodwill,
Which is but right, as God it wot:
    Forget me not.

Consider how I am your thrall
To serve you both in cold and hot.
My fault's for thinking naught at all,
In prison strong though I should rot.
Then in your ears let pity fall
And, lest I perish in your lot,
    Forget me not.

I love, loved, and so doth she
And yet in love we suffer still.
The cause is strange, as seemeth me,
To love so well and want our will.

O deadly yea! o grievous smart!
Worse than refuse, unhappy gain!
In love whoever played this part
To love so well and live in pain?

Was ever hearts so well agreed
Since love was love, as I do trow,
That in their love so ill did speed
To love so well and live in woe?

This mourn we both and hath done long
With woeful plaint and careful voice.
Alas, it is a grievous wrong
To love so well and not rejoice.

And here an end of all our moan!
With sighing oft my breath is scant
Since of mishap ours is alone
To love so well and yet to want.

But they that causer is of this,
Of all our cares God send them part
That they may know what grief it is
To love so well and live in smart.

Sometime I sigh, sometime I sing,
Sometime I laugh, sometime mourning.
As one in doubt this is my saying:
Have I displeased you in anything?

Alack, what aileth you to be grieved?
Right sorry am I that ye be moved.
I am your own if truth be proved
And by your displeasure as one mischieved.

When ye be merry, then am I glad.
When ye be sorry, then am I sad.
Such grace or fortune I would I had
You for to please however I were bestad.

When ye be merry why should I care?
Ye are my joy and my welfare.
I will you love, I will not spare
Into your presence as far as I dare.

All my poor heart and my love true
While life doth last I give it you;
And you to serve will service due
And never to change you for no new.

Absence! Absenting causeth me to complain,
My sorrow complaints abiding in distress;
And departing most privy increaseth my pain.
Thus live I uncomforted, wrapped all in heaviness.

In heaviness I am wrapped devoid of all solace.
Neither pastime nor pleasure can revive my dull wit.
My sprites be all taken and death doth me menace
With his fatal knife the thread for to kit,

For to kit the thread of this wretched life
And shortly bring me out of this case.
I see it availeth not, yet must I be pensive
Since fortune from me hath turned her face.

Her face she hath turned with countenance contrarious
And clean from her presence she hath exiled me,
In sorrow remaining as a man most dolorous,
Exempt from all pleasure, all worldly felicity.

All worldly felicity now am I private
And left in desert most solitarily,
Wandering all about as one without mate.
My death approacheth. Alas, what remedy?

What remedy, alas, to rejoice my woeful heart,
With sighs surprising most ruefully?
Farewell, all pleasure. Welcome, pain and smart.
Now welcome, death. I am ready to die.

I am ready and ever will be
   To do you service with honesty.
   There is nothing that lacks in me
     But that I have not.

My poor heart always and my mind
   Fixed in yours you shall still find.
   To love you best reason doth bind
     Although I have not.

And for your sake I would be glad
   To have much more than I have had,
   The lack whereof doth make me sad
     Because I have not.

For I do love ye faithfully
   And ye me again right secretly.
   Of let there is no cause why
     But that I have not.

If I you once of that might sure,
   Our love should increase and endure.
   To study therefore it is my cure
     How I might have.

Such are called friends nowadays
    Which do muse and study always
    Betwixt young lovers to put delays
        Because they have not.

But this resisteth all my trust, verily,
    That ye again will love me steadfastly.
    And let thy word pass, as it hath done, hardly
        Till that we have.

But for this time, sweetheart, adieu.
    Continue faithful and I will be true
    And love thee still, whatsoever ensue,
        Although I have not.

O, what undeserved cruelty
Hath Fortune showed unto me
When all my wealth, joy, and felicity
Are turned to me most contrary!

My joy is woe, my pleasure pain,
My ease is travail. What remedy?
My mirth is mourning, hope is in vain.
Thus all thing turneth clean contrary.

The place of sleep that should my rest restore
Is unto me an unquiet enemy
And most my woe reneweth evermore.
Thus all thing turneth to me contrary.

I burn for cold, I starve for heat.
That lust liketh, desire doth it deny.
I fast from joy, sorrow is my meat.
Thus every joy turneth to me contrary.

The place of my refuge is my exile.
In Disdain's prison desperate I lie,
There to abide the time and woeful while
Till my careful life may turn contrary.

Quondam was I in my lady's grace,
I think as well as now be you;
And when that you have trod the trace
Then shall you know my words be true,
    That *quondam* was I.

Quondam was I. She said for ever.
That 'ever' lasted but a short while.
Promise made not to dissever,
I thought she laughed – she did but smile.
    Then *quondam* was I.

Quondam was I – he that full oft lay
In her arms with kisses many one.
It is enough that this I may say:
Though among the moe now I be gone
    Yet *quondam* was I.

Quondam was I. Yet she will you tell
That, since the hour she was first born,
She never loved none half so l
As you. But what although she had sworn?
    Sure *quondam* was I.

I have been a lover
Full long and many days
And oft-times a prover
Of the most painful ways.
But all that I have passed
As trifles to this last.

By proof I know the pain
Of them that sue and serve
And nothing can attain
Of that which they deserve.
But those pangs have I passed
As trifles to this last.

I have ere this been thrall
And durst it never show
But glad to suffer all
And so to cloak my woe.
Yet that pang have I passed
As trifles to this last.

By length of time ere now
I have attained grace;
And ere I wist well how,
Another had my place.
Yet that pang have I passed
As trifles to this last.

My love well near once won
And I full like to speed,
Evil tongues have then begun
With lies to let my meed.
Yet that pang have I passed
As trifles to this last.

Sometime I loved one
That liked well my suit,
But of my deadly moan
Fair words was all the fruit.
Yet that pang have I passed
As trifles to this last.

My steadfast faith and will
With fair words have I told;
Yet have I found them still
In their belief to cold.
But that pang have I passed
As trifles to this last.

In love when I have been
With them that loved me
Such danger have I seen
That we would not agree.
But that pang have I passed
As trifles to this last.

Absence oft-times ere this
Hath doubled my disease
In causing me to miss
That thing that might me please.

Yet that pang have I passed
As trifles to this last.

To promise love for love
And make too long delays
Hath made me for to prove
Of love the painful ways.
Yet that pang have I passed
As trifles to this last.

Full many torments more
In loving I have found,
Which oft hath pained sore
My heart when it was bound.
Yet all that have I passed
As trifles to this last.

Now guess all ye that list
And judge now as ye please.
For oft-times have ye missed
In judging my disease,
Be nothing then aghast
Though ye misjudge these last.

Absence, alas,
Causeth me pass
From all solace
To great grievance.
Yet though that I
Absent must be,
I trust that she
Hath remembrance.

Where I her find
Loving and kind,
There my poor mind
Eased shall be.
And for my part,
My love and heart
Shall not revert
Though I should die.

Beauty, pleasure,
Riches, treasure,
Or to endure
In prison strong
Shall not me make
Her to forsake
Though I should lack
Her never so long.
For once trust I,
Ere that I die,

For to espy
The happy hour,
At liberty
With her to be
That pities me
In this dolour.

I must go walk the woods so wild
    And wander here and there
    In dread and deadly fear,
For where I trust, I am beguiled
    And all for your love, my dear.

I am banished from my bliss
    By craft and false pretence,
    Faultless, without offence;
And of return no certain is
    And all for your love, my dear.

Banished am I, remedies,
    To wilderness alone,
    Alone to sigh and moan
And of relief all comfortless
    And all for your love, my dear.

My house shall be the greenwood tree,
    A tuft of brakes my bed.
    And this my life I lead
As one that from his joy doth flee
    And all for your love, my dear.

The running streams shall be my drink.
  Acorns shall be my food.
  Naught else shall do me good
But on your beauty for to think
  And all for your love, my dear.

And when the deer draw to the green,
  Makes me think on a roe:
  How I have seen ye go
Above the fairest, fairest be seen!
  And all for your love, my dear.

But where I see in any coast
  Two turtles sit and play,
  Rejoicing all the day,
Alas, I think, this have I lost
  And all for your love, my dear.

No bird, no bush, no bough I see
  But bringeth to my mind
  Something whereby I find
My heart far wandered, far from me,
  And all for your love, my dear.

The tune of birds when I do hear,
  My heart doth bleed, alas,
  Remembering how I was
Wont for to hear your ways so clear
  And all for your love, my dear.

My thought doth please me for the while:
    While I see my desire
    Naught else I do require.
So with my thought I me beguile
    And all for your love, my dear.

Yet I am further from my thought
    Than earth from heaven above.
    And yet for to remove
My pain, alas, availeth naught
    And all for your love, my dear.

And where I lie, secret, alone,
    I mark that face anon
    That stayeth my life, as one
That other comfort can get none
    And all for your love, my dear.

The summer days that be so long
    I walk and wander wide,
    Alone, without a guide,
Always thinking how I have wrong
    And all for your love, my dear.

The winter nights that are so cold
    I lie amid the [storms],
    Unwrapped, in particular thorns,
Remembering my sorrows old
    And all for your love, my dear.

A woeful man such desert life
   Becometh best of all.
   But woe might them befall
That are the causers of this strife
   And all for your love, my dear.

Fortune, what aileth thee
Thus for to banish me
Her complay whom I love best
For to complain me
Nothing availeth me.
Adieu, farewell, this night's rest.

Her demure countenance,
Her homely patience
Hath wounded me through Venus' dart,
That I cannot refrain me
Neither yet abstain me
But needs must love her with all my heart.

Long have I loved her,
Oft have I prayed her.
Yet, alas, she through disdain
Nothing regards me
Nor yet rewards me
But lets me lie in mortal pain.

Yet shall I love her still
With all my heart and will
Wheresoever I ride or go.
My heart, my service,
Afore all ladies',
Is hers all only and no moe.

She hath my heart and ever shall
　　In this terrestrial.
What can she more of me require?
　　Her whom I love best,
　　God send her good rest
And me heartily my whole desire.

Love hath again
Put me to pain
And yet all is but lost.
I serve in vain
And am certain
Of all misliked most.

Both heat and cold
Doth so me hold
And cumbers so my mind
That, when I should
Speak and be bold,
It draweth me still behind.

My wits be past,
My life doth waste,
My comfort is exiled.
And I in haste
Am like to taste
How love hath me beguiled.

Unless that right
May in her sight
Obtain pity and grace,
Why should a wight
Have beauty bright
If mercy have no grace?

Yet I, alas,
Am in such case
That back I cannot go
But still forth trace
A patient pace
And suffer secret woe.

For with the wind
My fired mind
Doth still increase in flame.
And she unkind
That did me bind
Doth turn it all to game.

Yet can no pain
Make me refrain
Nor here nor there to range.
I shall retain
Hope to attain
A heart that is so strange.

But I require
The painful fire
That oft doth make me sweat
For all my hire
With like desire
To give her heart a heat.

Then shall she prove
   How I her love
And what I have her offered,
   Which should her move
   For to remove
The pain that I have suffered.

   A better fee
   Than she gave me
She shall of me attain;
   For whereas she
   Showed cruelty
She shall my heart obtain.

A NOTE ON SIR THOMAS WYATT

Sir Thomas Wyatt (1503-42) is generally seen as a very good poet, but perhaps not a 'great' one. He is not quite included in that celebrated pantheon of 'great poets': William Shakespeare, Edmund Spenser, William Wordsworth and John Keats. Wyatt is not quite in that realm, though he is certainly regarded as being in the second tier of major poets, that realm inhabited by Henry Vaughan, John Clare, Michael Drayton and Elizabeth Browning. C.S. Lewis's response to Wyatt is typical of general criticism of the poet:

> Wyatt remains, if not the finest, yet much the purest example of the plainer manner, and in reading his songs, with their conversational openings, their surly (not to say sulky) defiances, and their lack of obviously poetic ornaments, I find myself again and again reminded of Donne. But of course he is a Donne with most of the genius left out. Indeed, the first and most obvious achievement of the younger poet is to have raised this kind of thing to a much higher power; to have kept the vividness of conversation where Wyatt too often had only the flatness; to sting like a lash where Wyatt merely grumbled.[1]

It's a bit severe, isn't it, calling Thomas Wyatt 'Donne with most of the genius left out'. Terms such as 'genius' are rarely used in literary criticism these days; and anyway, C.S. Lewis's criticism is largely discredited.

One can see Wyatt's love poetry wholly in terms of Petrarchan poetics, if one wishes. Wyatt is, like Petrarch, very much a courtly love poet, a poet who professes, in his lyrics, the ethics of chivalry and courtesy. Like the troubadours, the Minnesangers

---

1 C.S. Lewis: "Donne and Love Poetry in the Seventeenth Century", in *Seventeenth Century Studies Presented to Sir Herbert Grierson*, Clarendon Press 1938

and the *stilnovisti*, Wyatt aims for poetic refinement, codes of honour, nobility, loyalty and pride; like Bernard de Ventadour, Giraut de Borneil, Petrarch, Guido Guinicelli and Dante, Wyatt writes at length of the beloved, espousing the traditional and so familiar notions of heterosexual, bourgeois romantic love. His yearning poet offers total devotion to the beloved woman, much as the saint kneels before the Virgin Mary. 'For yours I am' he writes ("My sweet, alas, forget me not"), 'Long have I loved her' he notes ("Fortune, what aileth thee"), 'I am yours assuredly' he claims ("The knot which first my heart did strain"), 'I was your thrall' he states in "Ye know my heart, my lady dear" . This is the language of loyalty and servitude that Shakespeare explored so bitterly and ironically in his *Sonnets*. In Wyatt's poesie, this thralldom is serious and relatively unquestioned; Shakespeare, though, restlessly questions the notion of worshipping the beloved, emphasizing the sadomasochistic aspects of the lover-beloved relation. Shakespeare comments harshly and often bawdily on the master/ mistress-slave relation, while Wyatt pretty much accepts it as it is. For Wyatt, the relation of mistress to lover is still noble, echoing the relation of knight or vassal to a lord, and saint to God.

What powers Wyatt's love poetry is loss of love, knowing the beloved once and now being estranged from her. Pain is the central experience in Wyatt's lyrics, the pain of not being with the beloved woman. She is elsewhere, so the poet consoles himself by writing poetry. Poetry is no consolation, though, and the more he writes the more dejected he becomes. As with Petrarch in his *Rime Sparse*, Wyatt in his love lyrics exacerbates and exaggerates the pain of love by making poetry out of it.

Thomas Wyatt employs the Petrarchan conceit at length. His images are, typically, of fire and ice, of burning and freezing, of love and loss. This passage from "At last withdraw your cruelty" is typical of Wyatt's Petrarchan imagery:

> For to the flame wherewith I burn
>   My thought and my desire,
> When into ashes it should turn
> My heart by fervent fire
> You send a stormy rain
> That doth it quench again...

Each Wyatt love poem sets up oppositions: the presence of the lover against the absence of the beloved; the cold winter of agonizing loss outside the body against the hot summer of burning desire inside the lover, and so on. Wyatt's protagonist lives in eternal sexual hardship:

> I toss, I turn, I sigh, I groan.
> My bed me seems as hard as stone
> ...For heat and cold I burn and shake...

He writes in "What means this when I lie alone?", while in "The joy so short" he groans of 'endless pain'. At times, Wyatt sounds more like Petrarch than Petrarch himself. The continuity between Petrarch and Wyatt is emphasized by the fact that Wyatt translated Petrarch. Indeed, it was Wyatt, some claim, who introduced the courtly love/ *stilnovisti* sonnet form into British poetry. Michael Spiller writes:

> the very first British writer to use the sonnet, Sir Thomas Wyatt, altered it very considerably: he made the first formal change in the structure of the sonnet since its invention in southern Italy in the early thirteenth century. [2]

Spiller then goes to discuss Wyatt's formal innovations, which included

> the alteration of the sestet from 3 + 3 to 4 + 2, ending with a rhymed couplet. It seems most probable that Wyatt, working with the *strambotti* of Srafino, was impressed by their epigrammatic neatness, and as a means of enforcing the wit and elegance of his own sonnets transferred the concluding couplet to his versions of Petrarch. (ib., 85)

Wyatt's versions of the *Rime Sparse* read like archetypal English love poems. He made Petrarch's sonnets more ambiguous and abstract.[3] Wyatt's Petrarchan poems became the foundations of the Elizabethan sonnets. His version of Petrarch's sonnet 134 – "I find no peace" (p.4) – reads thus:

> Pace non trobo e non ho da far guerra;
> E temo e spero, et ardo e sono un ghiaccio.

> I fynde no peace and all my warr is done;
> I fere and hope, I burne and friese like yse.

---

2 Michael R.G. Spiller: *The Development of the Sonnet: An Introduction*, Routledge 1992, 83-4

3 Spiller, 87; Anne Ferry: *The 'Inward' Language*, Chicago 1983, chapter 2

Compare the modes and images of Wyatt's love poems with Petrarch in, say, his sonnet (number 164) from his *Canzoniere*:

veggio, penso, ardo, piango; et chi mi sface
sempre m' e inanzi per mia dolce pena:
guerra e 'l mio stato, d'ira e di duoi piena,
et sol di lei pensando o qualche pace.

(I am awake, I think, I burn, I weep; and she who destroys me is always before me, to my sweet pain: war is my state, full of sorrow and suffering, and only thinking of her do I have any peace.)[4]

In Wyatt's poetry, we find the traditional ethics of Western culture: that love leads to pain, that pain is the true mark of love, that the greater the suffering the greater the love. This religion of love and pain (or sex and death as modern intellectuals call it) is found through poetry, from Petrarch through Wyatt, William Shakespeare and Maurice Scève, to John Keats, Charles Baudelaire and D.H. Lawrence.

This love-pain (sex-death) metaphysic finds its apotheosis in the work of Marquis de Sade. De Sade is the high priest of metaphysical eroticism, as later championed by Baudelaire, Jean Cocteau, the Surrealists, A.C. Swinburne, Lautréamont, Fydor Dostoievsky, Norman Mailer, Henry Miller, D.H. Lawrence and John Cowper Powys. Thomas Wyatt is very much a member of this illustrious pantheon of Sadeian artists.

Sir Thomas Wyatt's poetry plays out, in sophisticated modes, the sexism of patriarchal erotic art. The Sadeian philosophy of sex is fiercely heterosexual and heterosexist, and in Wyatt's verses the woman is definitely the object of male lust, simultaneously feared and desired. The history of poetry has its pornographic components. Look at the poems of Wyatt, Shakespeare, Dante, Petrarch, Paul Éluard, Robert Graves, Maurice Scève, Torquato Tasso, John Donne, John Skelton, etc. 'Woman' is the object of male desire in their poems. 'Woman' becomes synonymous with pain and death, in the noble experience of love. Poets emphasize the *pain* of love, the agony of desire. How I suffer for love of you! they cry, so many times in Petrarch's *Rime Sparse*, Dante's *Vita Nuova*, Shakespeare's Sonnets or Robert Graves' *Collected Poems*, and in the poems selected here in this book. In "If amorous faith", Wyatt speaks of 'sorrowful anger feeding busily', while in "The lively sparks that issue from

---

4 F. Petrarch: *Petrarch's Lyric Poems,* tr Robert M. Durling, Harvard University Press, Cambridge, Mass., 1976 164: 5-8

these eyes" he moans about 'the pain of my fall', and in "Like as the swan" he tells the beloved 'that you doth cause my death'.

Wyatt, like most male poets, tried to stylize the pain of love, but agony is inescapably a part of his form of erotic desire. Wyatt poeticizes in the manner of *fin amor*, where the beloved woman wounds the lover through the eyes with the arrow of love shot by Venus's phallic assistant, Cupid (he is 'wounded...through Venus' dart' in "Fortune, what aileth thee"). Dante wrote time and time again of this sensual wounding through the eyes in his *Divina Commedia*, as this extract from the *Paradiso* shows:

> Then Beatrice looked at me, her eyes
> sparkling with love and burning so divine,
> my strength of sight surrendered to her power –
>
> with eyes cast down, I was about to faint.[5]

Wyatt speaks at length of death, and of dying for love, dying for the beloved. In "Like as the swan" he cries 'I die! I die!', while in "What death is worse than this?" he writes that 'toward my death I drive'. Wyatt's yearning suitor seems always on the edge of dying, as if he carries a dagger ready to plunge (voluptuously, of course) into his aching heart. 'Now welcome, death,' he writes in "Absence! Absenting causeth me to complain".

In the male, Sadeian view, only painful sex is authentic. Throughout his poetry, Thomas Wyatt emphasizes his wretchedness, his burning/ freezing fever of love. Essentially, at this psychological level, Wyatt's poetry, like that of Shakespeare or Spenser or Dante or Petrarch, is no different from pornography. For one finds the same views in the works of pornography that one finds in Western love poetry. At this level of emotional pain and heterosexism, love poetry is no different from the major works of high class or 'literary' pornography: *The Story of the Eye, The Story of O, The Image, Tropic of Cancer, Lady Chatterley's Lover, The 120 Days of Sodom*, etc. Georges Bataille's *The Story of the Eye*, acclaimed by intellectual luminaries such as Jean-Paul Sartre, Susan Sontag, Michel Foucault and Peter Brook, is typical amongst intellectual pornography. The ethics it proposes – not secretly, not between the lines, not in the silences and spaces of the text, but upfront, in every sentence – are explained accurately by Andrea Dworkin: '[d]eath is the stunning essence of sex. The violence of death is the violence of sex and

---

5 Dante: *The Divine Comedy: Paradiso*, tr Mark Musa, Penguin 1986, IV: 139-142

the beauty of death is the beauty of sex and the meaning of life is only revealed in the meaning of sex which is death.'.6 The same emphasis on the 'love-death', as in the erotic death in *Romeo and Juliet* or the Arthurian legend of Tristan and Isolde, is found in Thomas Wyatt's poetry. In mediaeval and Renaissance love poetry, as in upmarket pornography, sex leads to death. The orgasm is the 'little death' (*petit mort*) and the most blissful way to die is at orgasm, where sex and death are conjoined rapturously and most poetically of all. The *'raptus'* of sex, the 'spasm', as men insist on calling the orgasm, is the experience that 'kills', and people 'die' in orgasm, Andrea Dworkin writes, and though she speaks of 'high class' pornography her reading here can apply to Renaissance love poetry:

> What matters is the poetry that is the violence leading to death that is the ecstasy. The language stylizes the violence and denies its fundamental meaning to women, who do in fact end up dead because men believe what Bataille believes and makes pretty: that death is the dirty secret of sex. (ib., 176)

The metaphysics of pain and sex and death and love are not confined to pornography or poetry. It is at the heart of Christianity, and Christianity is the most sacred of the Western world's institutions according to some people. Pain is glorified in Christianity in Christ dying on the Cross. The West does not exalt Christ's resurrection, his glorious rebirth so much as it exalts the awful suicide on the Cross. Wyatt's sacred lyrics do not veer from this view of the religious life as one made holy by personal suffering. But Wyatt, like his poet contemporaries, goes beyond religion, making love his religion or following. It's not about Christ's suffering, or gods, or organized religion, it's about men loving women, and poets loving women, and writing about it.

---

6 Andrea Dworkin: *Pornography: Men Possessing Women,* Women's Press 1981, 174-5

J.R.R. Tolkien
The Books, The Films, The Whole Cultural Phenomenon

by Jeremy Mark Robinson

A new critical study of J.R.R. Tolkien, creator of Middle-earth and author of *The Lord of the Rings, The Hobbit* and *The Silmarillion*, among other books.

This new critical study explores Tolkien's major writings (*The Lord of the Rings, The Hobbit, Beowulf: The Monster and the Critics, The Letters, The Silmarillion* and *The History of Middle-earth* volumes); Tolkien and fairy tales; the mythological, political and religious aspects of Tolkien's Middle-earth; the critics' response to Tolkien's fiction over the decades; the Tolkien industry (merchandizing, toys, role-playing games, posters, Tolkien societies, conferences and the like); Tolkien in visual and fantasy art; the cultural aspects of The Lord of the Rings (from the 1950s to the present); Tolkien's fiction's relationship with other fantasy fiction, such as C.S. Lewis and *Harry Potter*; and the TV, radio and film versions of Tolkien's books, including the 2001-03 Hollywood interpretations of *The Lord of the Rings*.

This new book draws on contemporary cultural theory and analysis and offers a sympathetic and illuminating (and sceptical) account of the Tolkien phenomenon. This book is designed to appeal to the general reader (and viewer) of Tolkien: it is written in a clear, jargon-free and easily-accessible style.

754pp   ISBN 1-86171-057-7   £25.00 / $37.50

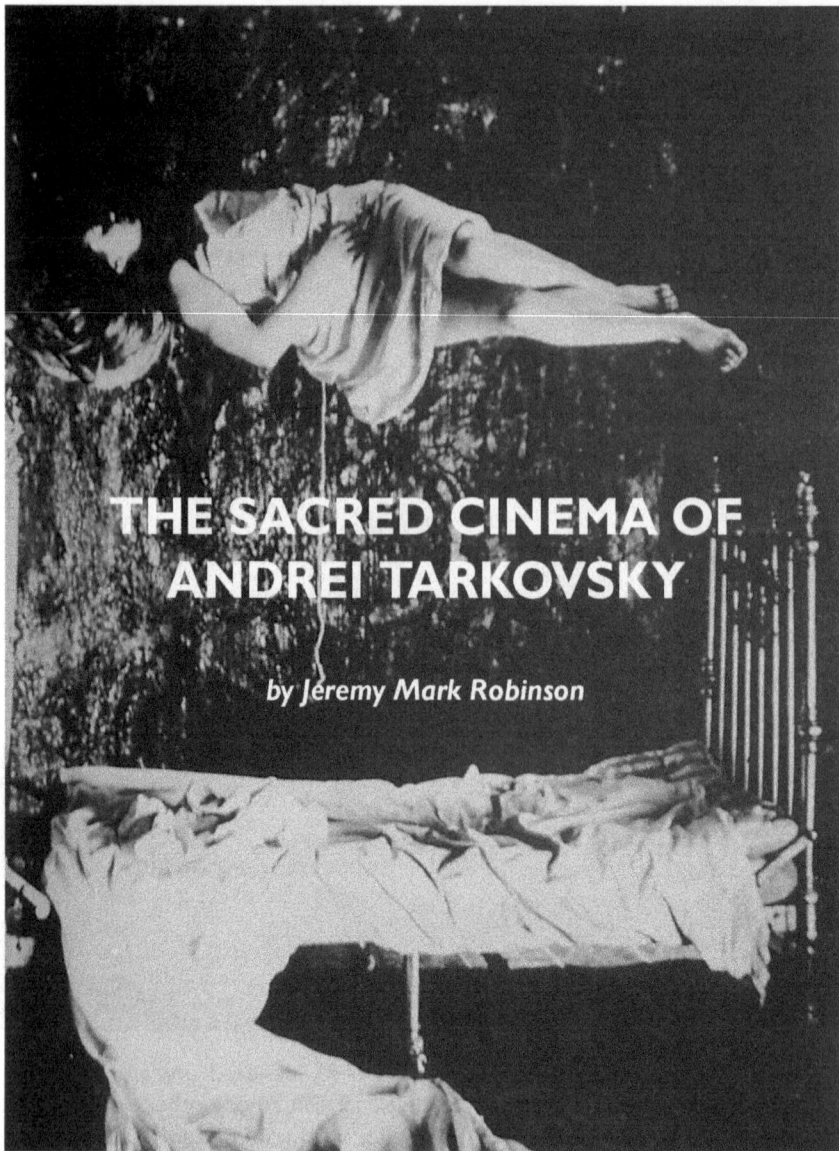

THE SACRED CINEMA OF
ANDREI TARKOVSKY

by Jeremy Mark Robinson

A new study of the Russian filmmaker Andrei Tarkovsky (1932-1986), director of seven feature films, including *Andrei Roublyov, Mirror, Solaris, Stalker* and *The Sacrifice*.
This is one of the most comprehensive and detailed studies of Tarkovsky's cinema available. Every film is explored in depth, with scene-by-scene analyses. All aspects of Tarkovsky's output are critiqued, including editing, camera, staging, script, budget, collaborations, production, sound, music, performance and spirituality.
Tarkovsky is placed with a European New Wave tradition of filmmaking, alongside directors like Ingmar Bergman, Carl Theodor Dreyer, Pier Paolo Pasolini and Robert Bresson.
An essential addition to film studies.

Illustrations: 150 b/w, 4 colour. 682 pages. First edition. Hardback.

Publisher: Crescent Moon Publishing. Distributor: Gardners Books.

ISBN 1-86171-096-8 (9781861710963) £60.00 / $105.00

The Best of Peter Redgrove's Poetry
The Book of Wonders

by Peter Redgrove, edited and introduced by Jeremy Robinson

Poems of wet shirts and 'wonder-awakening dresses'; honey, wasps and bees; orchards and apples; rivers, seas and tides; storms, rain, weather and clouds; waterworks; labyrinths; amazing perfumes; the Cornish landscape (Penzance, Perranporth, Falmouth, Boscastle, the Lizard and Scilly Isles); the sixth sense and 'extra-sensuous perception'; witchcraft; alchemical vessels and laboratories; yoga; menstruation; mines, minerals and stones; sand dunes; mud-baths; mythology; dreaming; vulvas; and lots of sex magic. This book gathers together poetry (and prose) from every stage of Redgrove's career, and every book. It includes pieces that have only appeared in small presses and magazines, and in uncollected form.

'Peter Redgrove is really an extraordinary poet' (George Szirtes, *Quarto* magazine) 'Peter Redgrove is one of the few significant poets now writing... His 'means' are indeed brilliant and delightful. Technically he is a poet essentially of brilliant and unexpected images...he never disappoints' (Kathleen Raine, *Temenos* magazine).

240pp   ISBN 1-86171-063-1   2nd edition   £19.99 / $29.50

Sex–Magic–Poetry–Cornwall
A Flood of Poems

by Peter Redgrove. Edited with an essay by Jeremy Robinson

A marvellous collection of poems by one of Britain's best but underrated poets, Peter Redgrove. This book brings together some of Redgrove's wildest and most passionate works, creating a 'flood' of poetry. Philip Hobsbaum called Redgrove 'the great poet of our time', while Angela Carter said: 'Redgrove's language can light up a page.' Redgrove ranks alongside Ted Hughes and Sylvia Plath. He is in every way a 'major poet'. Robinson's essay analyzes all of Redgrove's poetic work, including his use of sex magic, natural science, menstruation, psychology, myth, alchemy and feminism.
A new edition, including a new introduction, new preface and new bibliography.

'Robinson's enthusiasm is winning, and his perceptive readings are supported by a very useful bibliography' (*Acumen* magazine)
'*Sex-Magic-Poetry-Cornwall* is a very rich essay... It is like a brightly-lighted box. (Peter Redgrove)
'This is an excellent selection of poetry and an extensive essay on the themes and theories of this unusual poet by Jeremy Robinson' (*Chapman* magazine)

220pp   New, 3rd edition   ISBN 1-86171-070-4   £14.99 / $23.50

THE ART OF ANDY GOLDSWORTHY

COMPLETE WORKS: SPECIAL EDITION
(PAPERBACK and HARDBACK)

by William Malpas

A new, special edition of the study of the contemporary British sculptor, Andy Goldsworthy, including a new introduction, new bibliography and many new illustrations.

This is the most comprehensive, up-to-date, well-researched and in-depth account of Goldsworthy's art available anywhere.

Andy Goldsworthy makes land art. His sculpture is a sensitive, intuitive response to nature, light, time, growth, the seasons and the earth. Goldsworthy's environmental art is becoming ever more popular: 1993's art book *Stone* was a bestseller; the press raved about Goldsworthy taking over a number of London West End art galleries in 1994; during 1995 Goldsworthy designed a set of Royal Mail stamps and had a show at the British Museum. Malpas surveys all of Goldsworthy's art, and analyzes his relation with other land artists such as Robert Smithson, Walter de Maria, Richard Long and David Nash, and his place in the contemporary British art scene.

The Art of Andy Goldsworthy discusses all of Goldsworthy's important and recent exhibitions and books, including the *Sheepfolds* project; the TV documentaries; *Wood* (1996); the New York Holocaust memorial (2003); and Goldsworthy's collaboration on a dance performance.

Illustrations: 70 b/w, 1 colour. 330 pages. New, special, 2nd edition. Publisher: Crescent Moon Publishing. Distributor: Gardners Books.

ISBN 1-86171-059-3 (9781861710598) (Paperback) £25.00 / $44.00

ISBN 1-86171-080-1 (9781861710802) (Hardback) £60.00 / $105.00

CRESCENT MOON PUBLISHING

ARTS, PAINTING, SCULPTURE

The Art of Andy Goldsworthy: Complete Works(Pbk)
The Art of Andy Goldsworthy: Complete Works (Hbk)
Andy Goldsworthy in Close-Up (Pbk)
Andy Goldsworthy in Close-Up (Hbk)
Land Art: A Complete Guide
Richard Long: The Art of Walking
The Art of Richard Long: Complete Works (Pbk)
The Art of Richard Long: Complete Works (Hbk)
Richard Long in Close-Up
Land Art In the UK
Land Art in Close-Up
Installation Art in Close-Up
Minimal Art and Artists In the 1960s and After
Colourfield Painting
Land Art DVD, TV documentary
Andy Goldsworthy DVD, TV documentary
The Erotic Object: Sexuality in Sculpture From Prehistory to the Present Day
Sex in Art: Pornography and Pleasure in Painting and Sculpture
Postwar Art
Sacred Gardens: The Garden in Myth, Religion and Art
Glorification: Religious Abstraction in Renaissance and 20th Century Art
Early Netherlandish Painting
Leonardo da Vinci
Piero della Francesca
Giovanni Bellini
Fra Angelico: Art and Religion in the Renaissance
Mark Rothko: The Art of Transcendence
Frank Stella: American Abstract Artist
Jasper Johns: Painting By Numbers
Brice Marden
Alison Wilding: The Embrace of Sculpture
Vincent van Gogh: Visionary Landscapes
Eric Gill: Nuptials of God
Constantin Brancusi: Sculpting the Essence of Things
Max Beckmann
Egon Schiele: Sex and Death In Purple Stockings
Delizioso Fotografico Fervore: Works In Process 1
Sacro Cuore: Works In Process 2
The Light Eternal: J.M.W. Turner
The Madonna Glorified: Karen Arthurs

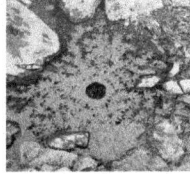

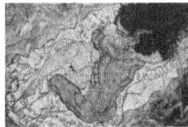

LITERATURE

J.R.R. Tolkien: The Books, The Films, The Whole Cultural Phenomenon
Harry Potter
Sexing Hardy: Thomas Hardy and Feminism
Thomas Hardy's *Tess of the d'Urbervilles*
Thomas Hardy's *Jude the Obscure*
Thomas Hardy: The Tragic Novels
Love and Tragedy: Thomas Hardy
The Poetry of Landscape in Hardy
Wessex Revisited: Thomas Hardy and John Cowper Powys
Wolfgang Iser: Essays
Petrarch, Dante and the Troubadours
Maurice Sendak and the Art of Children's Book Illustration
Andrea Dworkin
Cixous, Irigaray, Kristeva: The *Jouissance* of French Feminism
Julia Kristeva: Art, Love, Melancholy, Philosophy, Semiotics and Psychoanalysis
Hélène Cixous I Love You: The *Jouissance* of Writing
Luce Irigaray: Lips, Kissing, and the Politics of Sexual Difference
Peter Redgrove: Here Comes the Flood
Peter Redgrove: Sex-Magic-Poetry-Cornwall
Lawrence Durrell: Between Love and Death, East and West
Love, Culture & Poetry: Lawrence Durrell
Cavafy: Anatomy of a Soul
German Romantic Poetry: Goethe, Novalis, Heine, Hölderlin, Schlegel, Schiller
Feminism and Shakespeare
Shakespeare: Selected Sonnets
Shakespeare: Love, Poetry & Magic
The Passion of D.H. Lawrence
D.H. Lawrence: Symbolic Landscapes
D.H. Lawrence: Infinite Sensual Violence
Rimbaud: Arthur Rimbaud and the Magic of Poetry
The Ecstasies of John Cowper Powys
Sensualism and Mythology: The Wessex Novels of John Cowper Powys
Amorous Life: John Cowper Powys and the Manifestation of Affectivity (H.W. Fawkner)
Postmodern Powys: New Essays on John Cowper Powys (Joe Boulter)
Rethinking Powys: Critical Essays on John Cowper Powys
Paul Bowles & Bernardo Bertolucci
Rainer Maria Rilke
In the Dim Void: Samuel Beckett
Samuel Beckett Goes into the Silence
André Gide: Fiction and Fervour
Jackie Collins and the Blockbuster Novel
Blinded By Her Light: The Love-Poetry of Robert Graves
The Passion of Colours: Travels In Mediterranean Lands
Poetic Forms
The Dolphin-Boy

POETRY

The Best of Peter Redgrove's Poetry
Peter Redgrove: Here Comes The Flood
Peter Redgrove: Sex-Magic-Poetry-Cornwall
Ursula Le Guin: Walking In Cornwall
Dante: Selections From the Vita Nuova
Petrarch, Dante and the Troubadours
William Shakespeare: Selected Sonnets
Blinded By Her Light: The Love-Poetry of Robert Graves
Emily Dickinson: Selected Poems
Emily Brontë: Poems
Thomas Hardy: Selected Poems
Percy Bysshe Shelley: Poems
John Keats: Selected Poems
D.H. Lawrence: Selected Poems
Edmund Spenser: Poems
John Donne: Poems
Henry Vaughan: Poems
Sir Thomas Wyatt: Poems
Robert Herrick: Selected Poems
Rilke: Space, Essence and Angels in the Poetry of Rainer Maria Rilke
Rainer Maria Rilke: Selected Poems
Friedrich Hölderlin: Selected Poems
Arseny Tarkovsky: Selected Poems
Arthur Rimbaud: Selected Poems
Arthur Rimbaud: A Season in Hell
Arthur Rimbaud and the Magic of Poetry
D.J. Enright: By-Blows
Jeremy Reed: Brigitte's Blue Heart
Jeremy Reed: Claudia Schiffer's Red Shoes
Gorgeous Little Orpheus
Radiance: New Poems
Crescent Moon Book of Nature Poetry
Crescent Moon Book of Love Poetry
Crescent Moon Book of Mystical Poetry
Crescent Moon Book of Elizabethan Love Poetry
Crescent Moon Book of Metaphysical Poetry
Crescent Moon Book of Romantic Poetry
Pagan America: New American Poetry

MEDIA, CINEMA, FEMINISM and CULTURAL STUDIES

J.R.R. Tolkien: The Books, The Films, The Whole Cultural Phenomenon
Harry Potter
Cixous, Irigaray, Kristeva: The *Jouissance* of French Feminism
Julia Kristeva: Art, Love, Melancholy, Philosophy, Semiotics and   Psychoanalysis
Luce Irigaray: Lips, Kissing, and the Politics of Sexual Difference
Hélène Cixous I Love You: The *Jouissance* of Writing
Andrea Dworkin
'Cosmo Woman': The World of Women's Magazines
Women in Pop Music
Discovering the Goddess (Geoffrey Ashe)
The Poetry of Cinema
The Sacred Cinema of Andrei Tarkovsky (Pbk and Hbk)
Paul Bowles & Bernardo Bertolucci
Media Hell: Radio, TV and the Press
An Open Letter to the BBC
Detonation Britain: Nuclear War in the UK
Feminism and Shakespeare
Wild Zones: Pornography, Art and Feminism
Sex in Art: Pornography and Pleasure in Painting and Sculpture
Sexing Hardy: Thomas Hardy and Feminism

In my view *The Light Eternal* is among the very best of all the material I read on Turner. (Douglas Graham, director of the Turner Museum, Denver, Colorado)

The Light Eternal is a model monograph, an exemplary job. The subject matter of the book is beautifully organised and dead on beam. (Lawrence Durrell)

It is amazing for me to see my work treated with such passion and respect. (Andrea Dworkin)

Sex-Magic-Poetry-Cornwall is a very rich essay... It is like a brightly-lighted box. (Peter Redgrove)

CRESCENT MOON PUBLISHING
P.O. Box 393, Maidstone, Kent, ME14 5XU, United Kingdom.
01622-729593 (UK) 01144-1622-729593 (US) 0044-1622-729593 (other territories)
cresmopub@yahoo.co.uk   www.crescentmoon.org.uk

www.ingramcontent.com/pod-product-compliance
Lightning Source LLC
Chambersburg PA
CBHW062017040426

42447CB00010B/2036